FINISHING LINE PRESS

www.finishinglinepress.com

Near Afar

poems by

Richard Wilkinson

Finishing Line Press
Georgetown, Kentucky

Near Afar

ACKNOWLEDGMENTS

"From The Earth to the Moon" first appeared on Creative Colloquy's literary
website in November 2021 www.creativecolloquy.com

While the majority of poems in *Near Afar* are new, several appeared in my
earlier chapbook, *Electricity, Chemistry, and Air,* self-published in 2020.

Publisher: Leah Huete de Maines
Editor: Christen Kincaid
Cover Art: Gretchen Wilkinson, Jenny Lake, Grand Tetons National Park,
Wyoming. Oil on canvas. Used with permission.
Author Photo: Gretchen Wilkinson
Cover Design: Elizabeth Maines McCleavy

Order online: www.finishinglinepress.com
also available on amazon.com

Author inquiries and mail orders:
Finishing Line Press
PO Box 1626
Georgetown, Kentucky 40324
USA

Contents

From the Earth to the Moon 1

Moonshadow 2

California on $5 a Day 3

Kobe, Japan 1972 4

Afar, Ethiopia 5

At the Elephant Orphanage 6

It's Been 57 Years 7

The Dolphin Stampede 9

The Bouquet 10

The Kiss: A Villanelle 11

At the Arboretum 12

How I became a neatnik in exactly 100 words 13

Dear Charlie, Love Chuck 14

The Balloon 15

On Reading Ozymandias at 14 16

The Littoral Mind 17

Eggs 18

The Lark Ascending 19

The Hummingbird's Perspective 20

Ringlorn 21

Praisesong for Silly Pleasures 23

Leap 24

Bainbridge Island, Then and Now 25

The State of Affairs Abecedarian 27

Vivarium 28

The Red Zone 29

Oaks 30

Rocky Ford Elegy 31

For Katie and Eric Iverson

From the Earth to the Moon

"Fly me
to the moon," Sinatra
sang. What a wonderfully nutty glorious
quest achieved through remarkable technical
wizardry notable for the skills of so many amassed
with such vital purpose, all mind-melded by a singular
dream. Miles upon miles of wire and plastics, fantastically
confabulated just so with screws, bolts and nuts too numerous
to count. Aluminum, titanium, and molded steel, fuel to flutter a
chemistry professor's heart, all assembled in mind-boggling com-
plexity, the recipe magically birthing a gigundo self-contained tube
on top of which sit three men who will soon be rocketed a gazillion
miles at supersonic speed to the heretofore untrod surface of our
planet's mysterious mate. What faith these men must have, en-
trusting their precious mortality to this unseen horde, this
anonymous legion, each with their own story of loss
and lust, heartache and hope. Who knew what so
many complicated souls could accomplish
when they put their heads and their
hearts to work? Really…who
knew? Who?

Moonshadow

Moonshadow
is Cat Stevens favorite
among the many songs he wrote
a big hit in the 70s

A celebration of life
sparked when he first saw
his shadow below a full moon
after life in light-polluted London

He shadow-hopped
transfixed by the lunar glow

From this came the refrain
m o o o o n s h a d o w
moonshadow

Those first chords
firing synaptic sparks
for people of a certain age

Each note bouncing off the present
lighting memory's flame
aching for innocence past

California on $5 a Day

It was a thing in the sixties
a nutty notion even then
to travel on $5 a day

"Europe on $5 a Day"
"The Caribbean on $5 a Day"
"California on $5 a Day"

That last one
beckoned
bidding welcome

Picture this:
A boy
his heart freshly broken by his first true love
a car (naturally)
       a 1967 lime gold Ford Mustang with low profile tires
       the steering wheel flipped aside when getting in or out
some cash
some time

And, of course, the book

A collage of adventure flowed
a vineyard where he worked for a week
an encounter weekend in Berkeley
a new love much older than he
a ruby bought at an ancient hotel
       in the foothills of the Sierras

All this on $5 a day

Kobe, Japan 1972

a hill above Osaka Bay

a full moon rising
just past dusk

an American girl
twenty

laughing like silly goats
we leap together
down
    the
        grassy
           slope
towards Kobe

my year in Japan half done
my future
an ocean of possibility

the arrow of the
moon's reflection

pointing
  the
  way

Afar, Ethiopia

Each breath
an echo of our birth
each breath
a link in the endless relay
that began on the African plain
where Lucy,
the mother of us all,
first stood
right here
right here!
near Afar

The mystical interplay
of blood brain and bone
electricity chemistry and air
the grid inside us sparking thought
the source still
of our cruelty and our kindness
the shallow and profound

Our laughs binding us to friends
even as our muscles
are bound to our bones

The epic chance
of improbable events
interacting just so
our most ordinary gestures
astonishing
like a startled bushbuck or bird

Our better selves pausing
to speak tenderly to another
wishing them well

At the Elephant Orphanage

On the outskirts of Nairobi
you'll find the most adorable scene
an orphanage for baby elephants

See them tumbling over one another
wallowing in the mud
their human attendant
swabbing them endlessly
keeping them cool
joining the play

Each baby has their
own attendant
at night they sleep
in the same shelter

But imagine
the baby's journey
from the shelter of
their mother's legs
safe from harm

The sharp cracks
of the poachers' guns
the brutal sawing
the bloody beginning

It's Been 57 Years

It's been 57 years
Since the HMS Bounty
Hailed into my view

It's sails snapping above the swells
As the great ship slammed
Towards the bright hills of Tahiti

It's bare-breasted women
Firing darts into my teenaged brain
Shot through with hormonal waves

A lad bereft
Longing for
Lasses in tropical seas

It's been 57 years
Since Mr. Christian rose
Before the odious Captain Bligh

Stood tall on the heaving deck
Spoke truth to power
Cleaving Bligh

From his benighted command
With such unswerving bravery
And well-turned phrases

Tahiti's jade hills
Setting the scene
So wonderfully distant

From the brown hills
Of Los Angeles
Awash in its busyness and flash

57 years since my callow mind
Leapt aboard the Bounty
Its sails cracking so sharply

I could hear their reports
As I read   mesmerized
By the South Pacific

Its cobalt horizon
And curvaceous landscape
My youthful timidity

Briefly suspended
By a fervid imagining
Of courage

Adventure
And nakedness
Alive on a distant sea

The Dolphin Stampede

Departing Dana Point bound for Catalina we witnessed a dolphin stampede. Dolphins upon dolphins leaping together, harmonizing in an aquacade of massive proportions, the Pacific's waves the floor for their watery dance. Whose idea was it to surge together? The dolphin king? Do dolphins even organize by hierarchy like we primates? If not, then where did the impulse first spark, inciting such exuberance, a wild display of balletic joy? The sky was clear and water feisty with the wind bulldozing swells before it. It was quite a spectacle, the stampede. I wonder if the dolphins debrief these exhibitions in their own squeaky way. Or do dolphins judge one another's performance? Are they so zen that pure acceptance is their norm? Not love, but close. Some scientists say dolphins are basically "nonhuman persons", better swimmers with bigger brains. Yet the stampede was something else—a synchronized undulation of mammalian flesh arcing in the sliver of space between the wine-dark sea and azure sky. No wonder they were smiling.

The Bouquet

The boy grips the limp bouquet
picked from weeds
thriving at the playground's edge
dandelions gorse aster

> Seven decades ago
> the leader of the Scottish Himalayan Expedition,
> Sir William Hutchison Murray,
> said this:
> *Until one is committed there is a hesitancy*
> *the chance to draw back*

A mysterious thread draws the boy
to his playmate, a girl
of whom he knows nearly nothing
but her blazing speed and spirit

> *Concerning all acts of initiation and creation,*
> *Sir Murray said*
> *There is one elementary truth:*
> *That the moment one definitely commits oneself*
> *then Providence moves, too*

Years before his first caress,
years before he stumbles into love,
there is this fleeting moment
frozen in time
when he turns
to the blazing-fast girl
and she smiles

The Kiss: A Villanelle

What a world we've made together
From that first electric kiss
We knew right then, didn't we

We launched our life with a cymbal crash
We didn't mess around (well, in truth, we did)
What a world we've made together

We never tire telling
Of that electerrific kiss
We knew right then, didn't we?

We've healed each other along the way
Yet the healing still goes on
What a world we've made together

Luck and love in equal measure
With a son we so admire
We knew right then, didn't we

Our laughter lingers longer now
Our path ahead a wonder
What a world we'll make together
We knew right then, we did

At the Arboretum

Wed just weeks ago
we amble beneath
pink-petaled blossoms
quaking above
the cheery cherry path

Profuse puffballs of color
their weight bending double
the speckled branches
create a rose blush divide
of grassy lane
from cerulean sky

How can this not portend
a warm welcome
to the wedded world
foretelling pink-petaled paths to come?

Great gulps of spring-fed air
embellish our walk
a million wind-rustled petals clap
their champagne pink hands
as if in celebration
cheering we newlyweds along

How I became a neatnik in exactly 100 words

If you were to visit my office, you may note how neat it is. Many do. You would feel welcome, safe, enjoying art from Africa. The Burkinabe batik is quite nice, two women in headscarves bent pounding maize and millet amid fat baobabs and squat round huts. Orderly…purposeful…calm.

A hundred years ago my grandfather met a redhead who was not his wife. Divorce followed, as divorces do. From grandmother's tears fury flowed, engulfing first my father, then me.

Boys should not grow up afraid. If they do, they will make a refuge for themselves. An office, for example.

Dear Charlie, Love Chuck

Great Grandfather Charles "Chuck", b. 1919 – d. 1979
Great Grandson Charles "Charlie, b. 2017

Dear Charlie,

How wonderful we share one name. It thrills me, it does.
I never met your dad, though I understand he is kind. Be
like him, not me. I was better once, had moments when I
embraced the wonder of the world. Life is tough enough
without the scars of the Great Depression to weigh you
down. Just what was so great about it? My mother and I
slipping hopelessly from one woebegone flat to a sadder one
still, our hearts sinking darkly each step down we took.

How I charmed your great grandmother Grace is the glory
of my life. What a doll she was. So loving, so kind. I wish you
an equally great mate when your time is ripe.

I loved art and fishing. Our summers on Balboa's beaches
before she died were the best years for us all. She died
though; an untimely death, as is said. Life pretty much went
to pot after that.

You will affect all those whose lives you touch. Make those
moments count. Deal with your pain; embrace it, then let it
go.

I wish I knew you. I wish I knew your dad. I wish I knew
your brother, too. I wish…

Love,

Your great grandfather Chuck

The Balloon

"Of all that we're asked to give others in this life, the most difficult to offer may be forgiveness."
—William Kent Krueger, *This Tender Land: A Novel*

The faded balloon fisted tightly
how many years has it been?
five decades? no, six

Yet still the balloon
and the barely there string
fuse with the fist as one

Letting go leaves only a fist

Nothing to nurture
the hooks gripping
the tender heart

Nothing to remember
what it meant when
crying for help
no one came

Yet what a gift
to be done
fanning fading embers

Slowly
        crackling fingers

                loosen   and

        the balloon
                                floats away

                                        in the breeze

On Reading Ozymandias at 14

> *My name is Ozymandias, King of Kings;*
> *Look on my Works, ye Mighty, and despair!*
> *Nothing beside remains. Round the decay*
> *Of that colossal Wreck, boundless and bare,*
> *The lone and level sands stretch far away."*
> *—[excerpt] Percy Bysshe Shelley, 1817*

Mrs. Ducharme reads the words
of a long dead poet

Me in the muddle of ninth grade confusion
with hormonal storms elbowing in

How Shelley's "lone and level sands"
pierced my well-fogged mind

Remains a mystery still
yet remembered decades hence

Picture the moment the mighty king
conceived his colossal Wreck

Such extravagant enchantment!
such certainty!

The futility of the monument
of which the poem speaks

Immortalized in words
that live on

The Littoral Mind

The littoral mind marking
the languid drift
from the half-awake life
between stirring and rising

Thoughts twirl
like leaves swirling
along a lazy stream

Nothing stays for long
or sticks

Words seep into consciousness
like tugs oozing vaguely into view
taking shape
then dissolving
into the thick mist

Nothing to reach for
nothing to achieve
no preening
no posing

Just gentle waves
lapping the shore
as the tide climbs
the sloping beach

Eggs

My wife wanted to paint a picture of an egg
like Rembrandt or other past master
It's hard
harder than hands

It's the egg's oblong shape, for one,
its glowing shell and shadows
depth
perspective
the horizontal plane

Lost in that impulse inborn
since faint faces first appeared
in ancient caves
she mimics the masters' confident strokes

Their mellow ambers
and luminous blues
their detailed attention
at the molecular level

She pauses now
a sunny day and gentle breeze
invite her to step away
the window framing
the still meadow
the quiet coop

Letting that last brush stroke linger

The Lark Ascending[1]

quivering strains
of a lone violin
shimmer above
the dun-colored lark
alone on the land

the lark climbing aloft
on feathery notes
curving on currents of air
with lark's-breath ease
above the mellow hills

wandering like that light violin
chased by a velvety flute
then horn
then clarinet
entwined like loving sprites
in wild embrace

yearning for a time that never was
by a folk song that never was
the final notes drifting to a feathery close
as the lark glides gently down

landing with such shivering grace
yearning yet for home

[1] "'The Lark Ascending' is a short, single-movement work by the English composer Ralph Vaughan Williams, inspired by the 1881 poem of the same name by the English writer George Meredith." Wikipedia

The Hummingbird's Perspective

The other day I saw a woman
hang a vial of sugar water in her garden
for me and my relations to enjoy

What a kind and gracious thing to do
with winter coming soon

Granted we
my relations and I
are quite the show
with our festive feathering
and fast-fluttering wings
beating fifty times per second
our joyous trick
of flying backwards

Our elegant beaks
and technicolor throats
entertaining by merely feeding

What a simple exchange
we nourish our benefactors
as we nourish ourselves

Both hearts brighten
as we fly away

Ringlorn

Ringlorn—adj. The wish that the modern world felt as epic as the one depicted in old stories and folktales.
—The Dictionary of Obscure Sorrows

Wouldn't a fanfare
be great to hear
when we succeed
at whatever we tackle?

A swelling of horns
engulfing the scene
punctuating our wins
with sonic thunder?

A soundtrack for one's life
that's what we're missing
a melodious background
to our humdrum affairs

A sweeping orchestral fulmination
by John Williams, say,
or Vangelis...
think *Jurassic Park*
Chariots of Fire

Just listen!

Bulging basses
foresee the mountain
of difficulties ahead
percussive tattoos for chores

Strings and woodwinds harmonize
foretelling budding love
ambient vibratos for naps

And each morning
a crescendo syncopates
as our feet hit the floor

announcing us
to the world

Praisesong for Silly Pleasures

at last, a day of sun
after a week of autumn rain

time to bring in the patio cushions
won't be needed till spring

but how to get these sodden clumps
from the roof deck to the garage

it's a straight shot from the deck
to the gravel driveway fifty feet below

I lay out my target
a blue tarp

take the eight flights deckward
genuflect to the mighty volcano

I lean over the railing holding cushion #1
aiming for the blue tarp I let the orange clump fly

dang   missed

what a lesson in aerodynamics
and hidden power

like a sharpshooter I adjust for windage
let fly again   another miss

what a fickle beast
this invisible breeze

ten cushions to go

such silly fun for a man
of my years and education

Leap

"The work of your life is the work you should be doing.
So I say leap before you look."
—Mary Tabor[2]

Leap
because I'll regret not leaping
there is nothing to lose and
so much to learn

Leap
because I'm at my best ever
what better way to apply my best
than in a setting where I cannot hide

Leap
because this is my chance
to catalyze kindness in settings
where hurt prevails

Leap
because to stay is to play it safe
withering into retirement
wondering

Leap
because when I've leapt before—
to wed, to father, to move up north—
my life grew that much larger

Leap
Because it's time to leap

2 Quoted in Laura Maylene Walter, "From Corporate to Creative,"
(*Poets & Writers*, September/October 2013)

Bainbridge Island, Then and Now

1942
Dread like a stone
slows each step
innocents banished
to a desert jail
far from Puget Sound

Overnight abandoning
the lives they built
hustled by bayonets
toward a ferry and
foggy future
shrouded in fear

2023
Today a shady park
with winding paths
marks the lane
the families walked

A memorial wall parallels
their final steps
the names of each family member
burned in the wood
honoring those
we banished then
but the fear? the despair?
that you'll have to imagine

1942
My friend Henry's name is on that wall
as are his brothers', mother's, dad's
what did they talk about
as that trudged toward the ferry?
did they talk? or did they each
walk on in their own silent gloom?

Later Henry was wounded in Italy
he came home to the desert corral
in which he and his family were herded
shrapnel fused to his calf
a purple heart on his chest

2023
Choices made by those
with hardened hearts
cast shadows
lasting centuries

If only leaf-strewn paths and
solemn sculptures
could undo
the sorrow sowed

"Nidoto nai yoni"
let it not happen again
etched in stone
at the park
on Bainbridge Island

The State of Affairs Abecedarian

Almost from the
beginning I counseled
calm
dialogue. "Feuding fuels
enemies," I said.
"Forgiveness fosters fellowship."
Governing is
harder than fighting, more difficult to
imagine a welcoming world where differing views are not
judged harshly, are treated
kindly,
lovingly, if you will.
Mercy and charity are the beating heart of community.
Nevertheless,
opposing forces
proffer
quick fixes,
rebelling without building,
solving nothing.
"To what end?" one may fairly ask.
Utter tragedy:
Valuing only the lives of like kind is
wishful thinking at best,
xenophobic at worst.
Yet all dreams stem from the same source, a wish for a bit of
zest and a good life.

Vivarium

The day I retired I saw a nurse log
resting on the forest floor
fresh shoots like arms upraised
drank deeply from the mulch of decay

New life emerging bravely
beneath the shade
of the nurse log's neighbors
fullness taking root
fed by a legendary past

Such abundance!
cedar saplings
moss and ferns
home to bugs and birds alike
a rainbow of greens
suckling the crumbling breast
the very air alive
with the joy of birth

Our work is like that
new futures formed
from old stories
of long dead heroes
and legacy practices
life force pulsing through
the weight of lost souls

The nurse log
giving life still
from her sacrifice

The Red Zone

Some years ago a New Yorker cover
featured a football field
as a metaphor for life
one end zone
birth
the other
death

I don't know how well the metaphor holds up
yet I now find myself twenty yards from the goal
the red zone in the sport's patois
that final stretch of possibilities and last chances

What's the play here, in the red zone?
The old switcheroo?
Four yards and a cloud of dust?
A Hail Mary pass
made in desperation
with a small chance of success?

I hunker down
a decision made
the next play clear

The crowd goes wild
a fanfare
as I dance my way
to the goal

Oaks

Emerson compared life
to awaking on the step
of an endless staircase
then in time lying down
some sixty steps above
each step a year
the ghostly stairs ascending still
into the infinite mist

Rilke wrote that life is the rest
between two notes

How might I end
on a high note
a friend once asked
He was speaking
of my retiring, yet…

Legendary cathedral builders
planted oak trees
beneath the gaze of gargoyles
to replace worn beams
five hundred years hence
Enchanting myth, yet…

What seed might I sow now
that will serve others
on steps unseen above?
What music might I make
that tomorrow's people may sing?

Rocky Ford Elegy

Each place has its language, like how the water moves,
and we have to learn to read it to find where the fish are.
—Ibrahim Khan on Quora.com

Such simplicity
Doug standing at a bend in
Rocky Ford Creek
three hours east of Seattle

The cool creek water
swirling between Doug's waders
the sharp bite
of a chill spring morning

Casting

A Goldilocks grip on the rod
not too tight
not too loose

How many times has he flipped that rod
first back swiftly just past
the zenith of the arc
above his head

Then a quick snap forward
the diaphanous line suddenly afloat
sketching a cloud or womanly hip
in the frosty air

Defying gravity almost
then gently   magically
resting the pheasant tail nymph
(or is it the bunny leech?)
On the quiet ripple just behind
that rock   over there
the one stirring the
creek bank pool

Outfoxing the rainbow
(he hopes)

No bite?

Repeat

Let us review what it takes to excel at his passion
       Skill
       Patience
       Focus
       And time

The Japanese call this *shinrin-yoku*
forest bathing
it's restorative   fosters wellbeing

I can see him still
Doug standing there
in Rocky Ford Creek

Repeating that cast
his grin when the rainbow bites
his friend Bill nearby
cheering him on

Their ghosts forever twinned
forever serene
at Rocky Ford

With Thanks

A direct line can be drawn from the 2013 Whidbey Island Writers' Conference in Washington state through Seattle's Hugo House writing center to *Near Afar*.

My wife, Gretchen, was instrumental in launching me along the poetical path when she suggested I attend the poetry sessions at the Whidbey Island conference. I figured I wrote prose all day—reports, emails, curriculum—and poetry might represent a change of pace that would be both refreshing and illuminating. It has been both.

I remain indebted to my wife, my first encourager and patient reviewer, and to Caitlin Scarano, accomplished poet and writing coach. Special thanks to Katie and Eric Iverson to whom this work is dedicated and at whose dinner table *Near Afar* was launched. I'm indebted, too, to longtime friends Lee Kaaren and Betty Matsushita for their valuable suggestions that made "Bainbridge Island, Then and Now" so much better.

What I enjoy most about poetry is the wordplay, discovery, and surprise inherent in the writing and reading of it. Lawrence Ferlinghetti wrote, "Poetry is the shortest distance between two humans." My hope is you will find *Near Afar* a fun and refreshing respite in these challenging times.

Richard Wilkinson
Tacoma, Washington

www.ingramcontent.com/pod-product-compliance
Lightning Source LLC
Chambersburg PA
CBHW030459100426
42813CB00002B/282